A Bush Theatr

C000040683

THE P WORD

by Waleed Akhtar

Opened on 9 September 2022
Bush Theatre, London

THE P WORD
by Waleed Akhtar

Cast

Bilal	Waleed Akhtar
Zafar	Esh Alladi

Creative Team

Director	Anthony Simpson-Pike
Set & Costume Designer	Max Johns
Lighting Designer	Elliot Griggs
Sound Designer	Xana
Composer	Niraj Chag
Movement Director	Rachael Nanyonjo
Assistant Director	Adam Karim
Dramaturg	Deirdre O'Halloran
Voice and Dialect Coach	Gurkiran Kaur
Costume Supervisor	Maariyah Sharjil
Production Dramatherapist	Wabriya King
Casting Director	Jatinder Chera
Production Manager	Ian Taylor for eStage
Company Stage Manager	Kala Simpson
Assistant Stage Manager	Tayla Hunter
Production Electrician	Chris Hepburn
Scenic Artist	Ilaria Ciardelli

With thanks to Cris Maranca for scenic support.

All other characters voiced by Zaqi Ismail and Gurkiran Kaur.

The Bush are proud to have worked with Micro Rainbow to realise this production. Micro Rainbow opened the first safe house in the United Kingdom dedicated solely to LGBTQI asylum seekers and refugees, and works to support them at all stages of the process. microrainbow.org

Cast

WALEED AKHTAR | BILAL
Waleed Akhtar is a writer and actor.

His theatre credits include *AI* (Young Vic); *A Thousand Splendid Sons* (Birmingham Rep and tour); *Flight* (Vox Motus/The Bridge); *What Shadows* (Birmingham Rep/Park); *Fracked!* (Chichester Festival Theatre tour); *The Kite Runner* (Nottingham Playhouse and tour); *Cold Calling: The Arctic Project, Back Down* (Birmingham Rep); *Wipers* (Leicester Curve); *Velocity* (Finborough); *RE:HOME* (Yard); *A Midsummer Night's Dream* (Tooting Arts Club); *Under 11's* (Soho); *Love Match* (Cheltenham Everyman); *Make and Model: Radar Festival* (Bush).

His television credits include *The Great* (Hulu); *Tyrant* (FOX); *Three Girls, Casualty, Holby City, Bucket, Dustbin Baby, Doctors* (BBC); *Edge of Heaven* (Hartswood Films); *Law and Order UK* (Kudos); *The Gym* (BBC Studios). Waleed's film credits include *Cruella* (Disney); *The Wedding Guest* (Revolution Films); *The Roads Not Taken* (Adventure Pictures); *Salmon Fishing in the Yemen* (Kudos Film); *Night Bus, 90 Minutes* (El Capitan); *Miss You Already* (Embargo Films); *Bruno* (Jeva Films); *The Intent 2* (Purple Geko); *Sparks and Embers* (Cinemagine); *Sidney* (BFI).

Audio credits include: *Tommies*; *My Son The Doctor*; *In Here*; *What The Papers Say* (BBC Radio 4).

Waleed is also a resident member of the Actors for Human Rights network and is a seasoned comedy improviser.

ESH ALLADI | ZAFAR
Esh Alladi trained at LAMDA and the University of Cambridge. He is an actor, writer and producer who is also a qualified doctor. In 2019, he won the UK Theatre Award for Best Supporting Performance for *Hobson's Choice* at the Royal Exchange.

His theatre credits include *An Adventure* (Bolton Octagon); *Out West* (Lyric Hammersmith); *The Argument* (Theatre Royal Bath); *Hobson's Choice, Wit* (Royal Exchange, Manchester); *Rutherford and Son* (Crucible); *Absolute Hell, The Beaux' Stratagem, Dara, Behind the Beautiful Forevers, War Horse BBC Prom, From Morning to Midnight, Romeo and Juliet* (National Theatre); *Twelfth Night* (RSC); *Lions and Tigers* (Shakespeare's Globe); *Nell Gwynn* (Shakespeare's Globe/ETT national tour); *A Midsummer Night's Dream* (New Wolsey); *The House of In Between* (Stratford East); *My World Has Exploded a Little Bit* (Tristan Bates); *The Wind in the Willows* (Birmingham Rep).

His television credits include *Red Rose, The Other One, Anthony, Casualty, EastEnders, Apple Tree House, Frankie* (BBC); *A Confession* and *Houdini and Doyle* (ITV).

Esh's film credits include *Still Life, The Leak, Ordinary Love*, and *Christmas at the Palace*.

Creative Team

WALEED AKHTAR | WRITER
Waleed Akhtar is a writer and actor.

He was a Michael Grandage Company Futures bursary winner in 2021. His most recent work includes *Kabul Goes Pop* (Brixton House/ HighTide/Colchester Mercury – UK tour) and a new commission from Audible as part of the Emerging Playwrights scheme. He created *Sholay on the Big Screen* supported by the Bush and *I Don't Know What To Do* at the VAULT Festival 2020 (Evening Standard Pick of the Fest). His short film *Lost Paradise* was produced by UK Film Council, and he has contributed material for BBC Radio 4's *Sketchtopia* and *Newsjack* and BBC3's *Famalam*.

ANTHONY SIMPSON-PIKE | DIRECTOR
Anthony Simpson-Pike is a director, dramaturg and writer whose work has been staged in theatres including the Gate, Young Vic and Royal Court. He is currently Associate Director at The Yard Theatre, was previously the resident director at Theatre Peckham and associate director at The Gate Theatre. Anthony is also a facilitator, working with young people and communities, having worked at the Gate, Royal Court, Young Vic, Globe, and National Theatre in this capacity.

Recent directorial work includes *Lava* by Benedict Lombe (Bush); *Living Newspaper* (Royal Court); *The Electric* by Vickie Donoghue (Paines Plough/RWCMD); and *The Ridiculous Darkness* by Wolfram Lotz (Gate).

As a dramaturg Anthony has developed multiple seasons of work for the Gate and The Yard as Associate Director. Recent dramaturgical credits include *Much Ado About Nothing* (RSC); *Samskara* by Lanre Malalou (Yard); *Hotline* with Produced Moon (Tron Theatre); *Dear Young Monster* by Pete McHale (Queer House); and *Coup de Grace* by Almudena Ramirez (Royal Court).

MAX JOHNS | SET & COSTUME DESIGNER
Max Johns trained in theatre design at Bristol Old Vic Theatre School and was the recipient of a BBC Performing Arts Fellowship in 2015. Prior to this he worked for a number of years as a designer in Germany. His most recent UK productions include *The Climbers* (Theatre by the Lake); *The Strange Undoing of Prudencia Hart* (Royal Exchange, Manchester); *Once Upon a Time in Nazi Occupied Tunisia* (Almeida); *King John* (RSC); *The Panopticon* (National Theatre Scotland); *Overflow, Strange Fruit, Rust* (Bush); *Heartbreakin'* (WLB Esslingen, Germany); *Buggy Baby* (Yard); *Yellowman* (Young Vic); *The Half God of Rainfall* (Kiln/Birmingham Rep/Fuel); *Urinetown* (Central School of Speech and Drama); *Wendy and Peter Pan* (Royal Lyceum Edinburgh); *Kes, Random* (Leeds Playhouse); *Utility, Twelfth Night*

(Orange Tree); *Fidelio* (London Philharmonic Orchestra); *Enron, Our Town* (the egg); *Birthmarked, Life Raft, Medusa, The Light Burns Blue, Under a Cardboard Sea* (Bristol Old Vic); *Hamlet* and *All's Well That Ends Well* (Shakespeare at the Tobacco Factory). Upcoming productions include *Sound of the Underground* (Royal Court).

ELLIOT GRIGGS | LIGHTING DESIGNER
Elliot Griggs trained at RADA.

Theatre work includes *Amélie the Musical* (Criterion/Watermill/UK tour); *Fleabag* (Wyndham's/world tour); *Jitney* (Old Vic/Headlong); *Purple Snowflakes and Titty Wanks, A Fight Against, On Bear Ridge, Yen* (Royal Court); *The Wild Duck* (Almeida); *The Lover/The Collection* (Harold Pinter); *An Octoroon* (Orange Tree/National Theatre); *Missing Julie* (Theatre Clwyd); *Ivan and the Dogs* (Young Vic); *Richard III* (Headlong); *Disco Pigs* (Trafalgar Studios/Irish Rep, NY); *Dry Powder* (Hampstead); *Pomona* (Orange Tree/Royal Exchange/National Theatre); *Queens of the Coal Age, The Night Watch* (Royal Exchange); *Missing People* (Leeds Playhouse/Kani Public Arts, Japan); *The Misfortune of the English, Last Easter, The Sugar Syndrome, Low Level Panic, Sheppey, buckets* (Orange Tree); *Hir* (Bush); *Lampedusa* (HighTide); *The Oracles* (Punchdrunk); *Feeling Afraid As If Something Terrible Is Going To Happen* (Roundabout @ Summerhall); *Psychodrama* (Traverse 2).

XANA | SOUND DESIGNER
Xana is a freestyle live loop musician, sound artist, vibrational sound designer, archival audio producer, audio researcher, spatial audio installation artist and theatremaker. Xana also develops accessible sound systems for spaces, is an sound arts facilitator and is a music tech lead at music research and development label Inventing Waves.

Theatre credits include *Strange Fruit* (Bush); *Everyday* (Definitely Theatre, NDT); *Who Killed My Father* (Tron Theatre); *The Trials, Marys Seacole* (Donmar Warehouse); *...cake* (Theatre Peckham); *Sundown Kiki, Changing Destiny, Fairview, Ivan and the Dogs* (Young Vic); *as british as a watermelon* (Contact); *Burgerz* (Hackney Showroom).

NIRAJ CHAG | COMPOSER
Niraj Chag is a London-based composer and artist whose work spans a wide range from albums, to TV and film scores, theatre and live events.

Niraj's television and film soundtracks have reached a worldwide audience. These include *One Night in Bhopal, Our Girl* (BBC1); Bafta & Emmy winning Simon Schama's *The Power of Art* (BBC Worldwide); *The Age of Terror*, Andrew Marr's *Darwin's Dangerous Idea, Origins of Us* (BBC2); *Sex and the City* (HBO); *The Rise of the Continents* (Discovery Channel) and *All in Good Time* (Studio Canal).

By contrast, Niraj's album work allows him to explore and bring to life his own narrative. Albums include the critically acclaimed *Along The Dusty Road, The Lost Souls* and *Mud Doll*.

Other work includes the score for the official Olympic Torch event on London's South Bank (SBC). Musical *Wah! Wah! Girls* (Sadler's Wells); The Olivier Award winning *Rafta Rafta* (National Theatre); *Much Ado About Nothing* (RSC); *Dara* (National Theatre); *Captive Queen* (Shakespeare's Globe); *The Ramayana* (Radio 4). In addition, Niraj has scored over twenty dance productions including Shobana Jeyasinghs *Classic Cuts* (Royal Opera House).

RACHAEL NANYONJO | MOVEMENT DIRECTOR
Rachael Nanyonjo is a movement director and choreographer.

Rachael's training includes BA Honours in Dance Studies (Roehampton University) and MA in Choreography (Middlesex University).

Choreography and movement direction credits include *The White Card* (Northern Stage and UK tour); *Purple Snowflakes & Titty Wanks* (Abbey Theatre and Royal Court); *Trouble in Mind* (National Theatre); *Love Reign*, *Changing Destiny*, *In a Word*, *American Dream* (Young Vic); *The Death of a Black Man*, *Either* (Hampstead); *Pigeon English* (Bristol School of Acting); *Cinderella* (Nottingham Playhouse); *Cbeebies* (BBC); *Spine* (UK tour); *Great Expectations* (National Youth Theatre at Southwark Playhouse); *Two Trains Running* (ETT/Royal and Derngate); *Does My Bomb Look Big In This?* (Soho/Tara Arts); *Babylon Beyond Borders* (Bush); *Macbeth* (Orange Tree); *The Jumper Factory* (Young Vic/ Bristol Old Vic); *Misty* (Trafalgar Studios); *Sleeping Beauty* (Theatre Royal Stratford East, nominated for the Black British Theatre Best Choreographer Award); *After It Rains* (National Youth Theatre); *Shebeen* (Nottingham Playhouse and Stratford East); Bernstein's *Mass* (Royal Festival Hall); *Twilight* (Gate); *The Divide* (Old Vic); and *Cover My Tracks* (Old Vic).

Directing credits include *Recognition* (audio play with 45North Ltd & Ellie Keel Productions); *Bobsleigh* (Old Vic Monologues); *Amazina* (Film); *An Alternative Musical* (National, for NT Learning as co-director); *Assata – She Who Struggles* (Young Vic, for Young Vic fresh direction); *2:1* (Kanzaze Dance Theatre at Rich Mix).

Choreographer screen credits include *The Statistical Probability of Love at First Sight* (ACE Entertainment); *CBEEBIES: Christmas in Storyland* (BBC); and *Pirates* (Hillbilly Films/BBC/BFI).

ADAM KARIM | ASSISTANT DIRECTOR
Adam Karim is a theatre practitioner working as an actor, director and acting tutor.

As Director: *Second Person Narrative* (Clapham Omnibus/RBSW).

As Assistant Director: *Sorry You're Not A Winner* (Paines Plough).

As an actor Adam has worked with: The Jamie Lloyd Company, Shakespeare's Globe, Manchester Royal Exchange, Nottingham Playhouse, Greenwich Theatre, Queen's Theatre Hornchurch, Tamasha, Arcola Theatre, Kali Theatre, RADA Festival, Stephen Joseph Theatre, English Theatre Frankfurt, ALRA South and The Hope Mill Theatre as well as screen work for the BBC and BFI.

DEIRDRE O'HALLORAN | DRAMATURG
Deirdre O'Halloran is the Literary Manager at the Bush Theatre, working to identify and build relationships with new writers, commission new work and guide plays to the stage.

At the Bush she's dramaturged plays including Olivier Award winner *Baby Reindeer* by Richard Gadd, *Lava* by Benedict Lombe and *An Adventure* by Vinay Patel.

Deirdre was previously Literary Associate at Soho Theatre, where she worked as a dramaturg on plays including *Girls* by Theresa Ikoko and *Fury* by Phoebe Eclair-Powell. She led on Soho Theatre's Writers' Lab programme and the biennial Verity Bargate Award.

As a freelancer, Deirdre has also been a reader for Out of Joint, Sonia Friedman Productions and Papatango.

GURKIRAN KAUR | VOICE AND DIALECT COACH
Gurkiran Kaur is a voice, accent and dialect coach from London. She received her BA in Drama and Theatre Studies from Royal Holloway, University of London before training as an actor at The Bridge Theatre Training Company. She has an MA in Voice Studies from The Royal Central School of Speech and Drama and is part of Freelancers Make Theatre Work's Dawn Chorus collective. Gurkiran works at a number of drama schools and with private and corporate clients. She is part of The Voice and Speech Teaching Associations' EduCore Leadership Team and serves as a Junior Board Member.

Coaching credits include *Extinct* (Stratford East); *Queens of Sheba* (Soho); *NW Trilogy* (Kiln); *How to Save the Planet When You're a Young Carer and Broke* (Boundless Theatre); *Best of Enemies*, *Chasing Hares* (Young Vic/Headlong); *Red Pitch*, *Favour* (Bush); *Lotus Beauty* (Hampstead/Tamasha); *Henry VIII* (Shakespeare's Globe); *Offside* (Futures Theatre); *Marvin's Binocular's* (Unicorn); *The Climbers* (Theatre by the Lake); *Finding Home* (Curve) and *Good Karma Hospital* for Tiger Aspect Productions.

MAARIYAH SHARJIL | COSTUME SUPERVISOR

Maariyah Sharjil is a designer and supervisor.

She is a recent first-class graduate from BA Design for Performance at the Royal Central School of Speech and Drama (2021). Before her design training, Maariyah worked at Sands Films as a costume constructor.

Her most recent productions include Assistant Costume Supervisor for *The Father and the Assassin* (National Theatre); Costume Designer for *The Key Workers' Cycle* (Almeida).

She has a passion for detailed research and often has an expansive reading list that inspires her work. The heart of her practice is turning the stories of minority communities and the diaspora into a visual language while also embedding historical and cultural themes into her work and designs.

WABRIYA KING | PRODUCTION DRAMATHERAPIST

Wabriya King's practice is to create a space and a format to hold people safely while they navigate their experiences in relation to the theatre's work. Wabriya has previously worked as a dramatherapist on *The High Table, Lava, Fair Play, Red Pitch* and *House of Ife* at the Bush Theatre, for shows at Soho Theatre, Stratford East, and is currently working with Hampstead Theatre, The Royal Court, and Paines Plough.

JATINDER CHERA | CASTING DIRECTOR

Jatinder Chera took a position at the Royal National Theatre, following his graduation from the Casting Certificate, at the National Film and Television School. Prior to this, he worked as an actor, having trained at Millennium Performing Arts.

For the NT, Jatinder cast *Up Next Gala 2022* (Lyttelton, choreography Stephen Mear).

As Casting Associate, he worked on *The Father and the Assassin* (Olivier, dir. Indhu Rubasingham).

As Casting Assistant, Jatinder worked on *Othello* (Lyttelton, dir. Clint Dyer), *Much Ado About Nothing* (Lyttelton, dir. Simon Godwin), *Small Island* (Olivier, dir. Rufus Norris), and *Trouble in Mind* (Dorfman, dir. Nancy Medina).

IAN TAYLOR FOR ESTAGE | PRODUCTION MANAGER

Ian Taylor is a Technical and Production Manager with over a decade of experience in the theatre and events industry. Ian has an extensive background in Stage Management and as Managing Director of eStage, a company dedicated to serving the needs of the entertainment industry.

His career began in Stage Management with Glyndebourne and the Royal Opera companies in 2004 and 2006, respectively, as an Assistant Stage Manager. Within a couple of years, he became a Stage

Manager for the Royal Opera, beginning with *Così fan Tutte* in 2010. Other companies he's stage managed for include ROH2, Secret Cinema, Opera Holland Park and Pimlico Opera. He was Senior Stage Manager for Opera Holland Park's Summer Festival for four years and, in 2012, started Production Managing for Hampstead Theatre, the Royal Opera, Southwark Playhouse, Park Theatre, the Philharmonia Orchestra, W11 Opera, Arcola Theatre, Troupe Productions, Papatango and Secret Cinema.

KALA SIMPSON | COMPANY STAGE MANAGER

Having trained at the Central School of Speech and Drama with over twenty years of experience, Kala Simpson has worked on a range of performances from West End to Rural Touring and has a passion for new writing.

Previous credits include: *Harm*, *Fair Play*, *Red Pitch* (Bush Theatre); *The Big Life*, *The Etienne Sisters*, *Room*, *High Heeled Parrot Fish*, *The Blacks* (Stratford East); *Medea* and *Romeo and Juliet* (Headlong); *The Hounding of David Oluwale*, *Sus*, and *One Monkey Don't Stop No Show* (Eclipse Theatre Company).

TAYLA HUNTER | ASSISTANT STAGE MANAGER

Tayla Hunter is a 2022 Stage Management graduate from the Royal Central School of Speech and Drama. She is really interested in working on a range of shows and productions as she starts her professional career, but she especially wants to work on BAME productions. She is open to working in film and television.

Tayla has most recently worked as an ASM on *Lotus Beauty* (Hampstead) and *A Place for We* (Park/Talawa, Olivier Award nominated and Offie Award winner for Best Ensemble).

Bush Theatre 50

EST. 1972

We make theatre for London. Now.

Celebrating its 50th Birthday in 2022, the Bush is a world-famous home for new plays and an internationally renowned champion of playwrights. We discover, nurture and produce the best new writers from the widest range of backgrounds from our home in a distinctive corner of west London.

The Bush has won over 100 awards and developed an enviable reputation for touring its acclaimed productions nationally and internationally.

We are excited by exceptional new voices, stories and perspectives – particularly those with contemporary bite which reflect the vibrancy of British culture now.

Located in the newly renovated old library on Uxbridge Road in the heart of Shepherd's Bush, the theatre houses two performance spaces, a rehearsal room and the lively Library Café & Bar.

Supported by
ARTS COUNCIL ENGLAND

h&f
hammersmith & fulham

bushtheatre.co.uk

THE P WORD

Waleed Akhtar

To Caryll

Characters

ZAFAR, *thirty-two, Pakistani*
BILAL/BILLY, *thirty-one, British Pakistani*

This text went to press before the end of rehearsals and so may differ slightly from the play as performed.

ACT ONE

BILLY. Knew it was on, the minute I saw his Instagram linked to his profile. He's a white boy who has been travelling to India...

ZAFAR. Haroon was always there. I don't remember a time before him, since we were kids we were inseparable.

He'd always pick me first when we played cricket.

I'm shit at cricket, he was brilliant, tall and strong. Could have played for Pakistan if he was given half the opportunity. But he came from a poor family in our village. By fifteen he was working in my father's factory. Never complained, always a smile on his face.

It's a cliché to talk about a smile that lights up a room, but it lit me up.

BILLY. Pictures of him outside the Taj Mahal, pictures of the curries he ate, on a beach with some local kids, in a rickshaw. That means he's down with a bit of brown. Plus I'm like the best version of brown. I'm not even into Pakis and I'd probably hook up with myself. Like you can't tell I'm Pakistani straight away, most people can't believe it when I tell them anyway.

My name gives it away... Like of all the names my parents could have given me, why not Adam? Daniel or I would even have settled for Zayne. They chose... Bilal. Fuck that, Bilal was the fat boy who got bullied at school for being a big brown poof. But Billy is the jacked masc lad, who gets all the boys.

He gets a Grindr message so pulls out his phone.

And this one's just sent me a picture of him bent over and his Calvins are nowhere to be seen. Can't wait, love me a twinky little white boy. Got to respond –

He begins to type a message.

ZAFAR. Doctors and nurses, another game we would play, a lot. Always give each other mouth-to-mouth resuscitation. Somewhere along the line we dropped the game and just the mouth-to-mouth bit remained. Kissing him, I would never want to stop.

BILLY. 'Nice' nah too ambivalent, 'sexy' too eager, 'hot' yeah that's the one.

And bingo I'm in. He's pinging me his location, practically begging me to come over, his housemate's away so he's got the place to himself.

BILLY *types.*

'I'll definitely cum, maybe twice.' What? It's subtle! (Don't hate the player hate the game.)

ZAFAR. It's nice to remember him like this. The real Haroon. Not the bit at the end. I don't want to remember that.

BILLY. I rock up to his apartment block, I knock and I'm nervous… No matter how many times you do this (and I've done this a lot) you still get that fluttering feeling in your stomach. Possibility, fear, excitement, dread all at the same time. The door opens.

Fuck, he's better looking than his profile pics, no one's better looking than their pictures, you always account for like a ten per cent margin of uglier than the profile.

But this guy.

Get it together, Billy.

ZAFAR. I don't have a single picture of him. I left Pakistan in such a hurry, the majority of my things are still there. I worry about forgetting his face. Sometimes it's this niggling feeling, just small. Other times I chide and berate myself for not being able to remember the exact position of the beauty spot on his cheek, the broadness of his shoulders, the slight bump on his nose.

'You do speak English right? You don't need a translator?'

I've been silent too long. I'm in the lawyer's office. The letter came today. The one that was supposed to set me free. Although it didn't.

BILLY. 'Whatsup.'

'Why don't you come in?'

'Sure sure.'

I walk in, offer to take my shoes off, sometimes the Pakistani slips out without even realising. He says it's fine. We end up chatting in his living room –

'Billy, what's that short for?'

'Just Billy.'

He doesn't push it, think he's woke enough not to ask me where I'm from.

Actually I'm enjoying the conversation. He works for a charity. Tells me about the half-marathon he did…

Don't do it, Billy! This is just a hook-up. Not a date. So I work my moves.

'It's a nice flat, wanna give me the grand tour… Why don't we start with the bedroom?'

ZAFAR. 'No I speak English.'

The lawyer looks at his clock. I had to wait two hours outside his office before they would see me.

'Will they send me back to Pakistan?'

'You will need to make an appeal.'

I can't go back, I won't go back. This bit was supposed to be easy, or easier. But my words weren't good enough for them once. What will change a second time?

BILLY. And we're on his king-size kissing and ripping each other's clothes off. He's peeling off my boxers.

'You're cut, so Muslim? Arab? Pakistani?'

Forgot my cock is the other thing that gives me away…

'Urmm yeah.'

'Don't worry I like Pakistani, like how they dominate, I can be a little sub.'

So I give him what he wants, act the part. Give him a little slap, choke him a little, tell him 'I own your fucking ass.'

He's loving it, can't get enough.

I mean I suppose I am too? Of course I am. He's hot… Look at him, he's toned, smooth, blue eyes, blond hair, perfect ass… white.

ZAFAR. Can't control my memories. The good ones, the bad ones, the ones they don't believe.

The noise in my head is constant. Gets louder at night.

They gave me pills to sleep, and when I get up in the morning there is this moment between sleep and wake. Where the reality of Hounslow and the filthy accommodation I'm in hasn't sunk in.

Can almost feel him, like nothing ever happened. Like he's there next to me.

The letter from the Home Office. Application rejected. Insufficient proof. After all that waiting. After everything I had to endure, and continue to. They didn't find me credible.

The solicitor says I have to pay him to make an appeal. I have no money.

Right now I long for that moment, the gap between sleep and awake.

BILLY. We've been spooning for ages. Feels good. Lying here in the afterglow.

He falls asleep. Does this cute little snoring thing.

Do I snore? I don't know, don't really sleep with anyone else, like I sleep with people but not *sleep* sleep.

When I go to leave, we kiss at the door for ages, he's a good kisser. I get the feeling he wants me to stay. But I tell him I have to go.

ZAFAR. I feel drowsy.

Lie down on the single bed in my box of a room.

The pills are kicking in. I took more than I was supposed to, but they don't bring peace.

I'm back at Lahore Airport, walking towards the desk. Constant announcements on the tannoy putting me on edge, strip-lighting making my head pound.

Hand over the passport, my brother's passport, to the woman behind the desk. We kind of look alike, but his features are rounder, his nose more pronounced, his face… still intact.

My heart is pounding hard. The pain in my head so intense like my brain could explode, sending bits of me splattering onto her Pakistan International Airlines uniform.

She's inspects the visa stamp.

My breath quickens, with every inhale my ribs ache.

Still has three months valid from when my brother went to Birmingham for a work conference.

She turns to the page with the photograph.

Should I puff out my cheeks a little, make myself rounder? She just waves me past.

I mutter a thanks to God, at least that's one prayer listened to.

Eventually when I'm thousands of feet in the sky I breathe normally. That's when I begin to cry – ugly, snotty, guttural – from the depths of my soul.

The old man sitting next to me turns and asks:

'Is everything okay?'

'Someone has died.'

'Who, beta?'

'The love of my life.'

His eyes turn sad.

'Sabar. [Fortitude.] May Allah grant it you. I lost my wife after fifty years of marriage. But to Allah we belong and to Allah we shall return.'

I cry even harder at this stranger's kindness.

And then it occurs to me, if this sweet old man knew that I loved a man and not a woman would he want me dead too?

BILLY. For days afterwards all I can think is how nice it would be to have someone. Waking up with him on the regular, spoil him, make him breakfast in bed.

I'd be a fucking great boyfriend. I think I would, if I had the chance. I don't know 'cause I've never really... You know.

ZAFAR. I take more of the pills. I'm still in the haze of searching for him. Then his face, his beautiful face. There you are, Haroon. Finally.

He looks so handsome as a groom.

Watching the person you love marry someone else breaks you in ways you didn't know possible. Makes you fear your face will expose you. Makes you wish death on a woman you've never met.

I walk towards Haroon, every step an affront to my need to turn and run.

I mutter a congratulations to his bride, not looking at her face.

And as is customary, we hug, my flesh pressed up against his. Not sure I have it in me to ever release him.

But eventually I do.

I turn and my father is behind me. He looks at me directly in the eyes, a panic rises in me.

'Now your childhood friend has become a man, you'll be next.'

I want Haroon again, not him.

I take more pills.

And finally he is right next to me. My Haroon, the intensity of his eyes fixed directly on me, the warmth of his body as he leans in to kiss me. And then... nothing.

BILLY. Me and Mark, yeah that's his name, have hooked up three times now. This might be a thing you know.

We've been texting a bit too since. Last one was from him yesterday morning.

I sent: 'Let me know when you want a repeat.' He said: 'Definitely will do. Kiss kiss.' Then I replied with a 'kiss kiss' so technically I was the last one to reply but a kiss isn't a reply. It's just not being rude, right?

Like what the fuck, it doesn't matter who texts who, and when. We're not fucking schoolgirls. Right?

Pulls his phone out and sends a message.

'How's your day been, sexy?'

He puts his phone away.

Time to get on with my own day.

First up, gym. Today is legs, never skip legs, it's the foundation. Plus is there anything worse than chicken legs? Just gonna get the workout playlist on the go.

Pulls out his phone.

Two blue ticks... (so he's read the message).

This playlist has more Olivia Rodrigo than I care to admit. I'm getting my pump on, loading up the squat rack. Some fag is checking me out, he's alright, but I have a golden rule: never fuck anyone at the gym. Gets awkward the next time you need to work out.

I'm done… Protein shake.

He's not replied yet. He's probably working.

That's where I should be too (work). Creative Executive for a bunch of internet fashion brands. Soon to be Senior Creative. Well, I mean I should be, I'm practically doing the job already.

ZAFAR. The doctor sitting opposite me is wearing a hijab. I know it shouldn't but it makes me uncomfortable in a way it never did before. Scared of how she will judge me, while I judge her.

'Would you like to talk about anything?'

She has a kind face, I don't want to see it turn bitter towards me. I stay silent.

'You took a very drastic step.'

She means swallowing the whole packet of sleeping pills. I want to tell her I wasn't necessarily thinking about killing myself.

'You can talk to me about anything.'

I'm exhausted from constantly assessing people, level of threat they pose, how will they react, who can I trust. Some days it's so bad I walk around Hounslow afraid of every brown face. Paranoid that I might be known or there may be a connection to my father. Even though we have no family here. In the temporary accommodation I don't talk to anyone, it's better that way. Better that they don't know about me.

But I need help. Alone. I have no other options. So I begin and she listens.

Her kind face remains kind.

'The Home Office said I wasn't credible, they didn't believe that I had been tortured or that I was gay. So as far as they are concerned I can go back to Pakistan.'

She looks shocked.

'I waited for a whole year, and they didn't believe me. And then my lawyer was asking for money, for them to make an appeal for me, money that I don't have. I have to live off forty pounds eighty-five a week. I've never been this poor... look at what I'm wearing. That's when I did what I did.'

'I believe you, and I'm sorry you had to go through any of this.'

Those few words mean so much. She writes numbers down on a piece of paper. Charities that support LGBT-plus people. That's what I am now.

This appointment was only supposed to be ten minutes. Not sure how long we have been talking. As I leave she touches my arm, it's the most human contact that I have had in months.

'If you ever feel like that again you come to me straight away.'
Later, I realise she slipped twenty pounds into my pocket.
I was expecting every other reaction but not kindness.

BILLY. The morning is spent in meeting after meeting.

Check my phone. He still hasn't messaged me back.

We spend more time talking about work than actually doing work. We're gearing up for Pride, the organisation wants a big push of love for the LGBT-plus community, apparently 'there's still loads of money to be made from the pink pound'.

Meeting's nearly over and I'm reaching for my phone when Fat Jason speaks up. Why? We were nearly out the door.

I used to think Jason might be fit if he cut his hair and went to the gym. But the thing with Jason is, even if he did lose all that weight, he'd still be a pretentious prick.

He's in full flow about how 'Pride is not really an inclusive space, maybe we should be looking to support in other ways.' All eyes are on me, the only POC in the room.

'I think Pride's a great idea.'

My boss smiles.

We do a working lunch, as if we need to talk more. Jason won't shut up... he's going on and on about giving up carbs. Now work is forcing him to go to Pride, he's only got a few weeks to get into shape.

He checks his phone.

And Fat Jason's still talking with his fat mouth.

'It's gonna take more than a few weeks to lose all of that.'

Everyone at the table turns to look at me. One of the girls laughs. Jason looks like he's been punched.

What? It's fucking true and at least he shuts up.

ZAFAR. The time difference is four hours so she would still be at home alone. I dial the number. It rings and rings. And with every ring I lose my resolve... What if he answers?

BILLY. Back to work.

Nothing.

Drinks after work.

Nothing.

Bus home.

Nothing!

How long does it fucking take to respond to a fucking text?

ZAFAR. I am about to hang up.

'Assalamualaikum.'

It's her. The last time I heard her voice she was bundling my broken body into a car with my brother's passport, telling me to get as far away as possible.

'Waalaikumsalam.'

Silence.

'It's me, Zafar... Your son.'

Silence.

'I don't have a son by that name and I don't know a Zafar. Don't ever call here again.'

The phone goes dead.

BILLY. Ghosted.

ZAFAR. Nervous, I walk into the room. I mainly came for the free lunch. Now I'm sat with six other men. Each has their own story.

Damba and David from Uganda,

Reza from Iran,

Omar from Nigeria,

Arsen from Kazakhstan,

Fyzal from Pakistan like me, but older, much older.

Each one of us is gay and had to flee here for our lives. It's a peer-to-peer support group, counselling had a year-long wait. So this was all they could offer. I don't speak much at first, I just listen.

BILLY. Been hitting the gym hard. More I push, less I think. It's Saturday evening, I'm the only one here.

I sent him another message the day before last.

'Is everything okay?'

Even as I press send I know, but still I do it.

Two days, nothing.

Idiot. I'm a fat fucking ugly idiot.

Push myself to do another set – 'Come on you pathetic piece of shit.' I fail. Fuck this.

ZAFAR. Damba has just finished sharing to the group. Five years in the system. Not knowing, not being able to work, stuck. Waiting on an appeal.

I pray not to be Damba. I speak:

'Even criminals know how long their sentence is. From the moment we get here we're treated worse than criminals.'

Clive who runs the group encourages me to share. So I do:

Two border guards in uniform, the bald one is angry.

'There's no war in Pakistan, no one is trying to kill you. You lot always trying it.'

The other one not speaking looks like he could be an uncle of mine.

I want to say they are playing good cop, bad cop, but I'm not a criminal. So why are they treating me like one?

'My life is under threat… My father and other men… They want… to kill me. It's not safe for me there.'

'Sometimes I want to kill my kids; it doesn't mean they get to seek asylum.'

'They killed my friend. My best friend. We were more than friends.'

I catch Uncle's eye.

'Are you saying he was your boyfriend?'

He looks down.

'We were in love.'

'Are you saying you're a homosexual?'

'Yes. Yes I am…'

'Top or bottom?'

'Are you the one giving it or are you the one who's getting it?'

I look toward Uncle.

'You need to answer his questions.'

'I don't think you're gay, I think you're making it up.'

'Why? Why? Would I make this up?' I point out my bruises.

'They could be from anything. Up, get up and walk.'

He gets up and walks.

'See, you don't walk like a gay.'

'But I am. I am… a gay.'

BILLY. Get home, down another protein shake.

No plans this evening and I don't want to be alone.

He opens up Grindr.

All the available fags within the vicinity. Some of the same
faces I've seen on here for years,

And here I am once again… Grinding away.

I'm back in front of another door, there's less excitement this
time, less hope. He (I don't know his name) opens it. He's
exactly what I was looking for.

Ugly and old.

I can already see it in his eyes, he looks like he's hit the
jackpot. Makes me feel good. Strut right in, no need to be
polite. He tries to make chit-chat –

'I'm not here to talk.'

We move directly to his bedroom. He kisses me, tells me
how beautiful I am, how much he loves my skin and my
colouring. I don't say anything back, no need to lie to him…
we both know the truth. He tells me he likes it when a guy's
in control. So I say:

'Shut up and get on all-fours.'

'Yes, sir, you can be as rough as you like. Hit me if I fail to
please.'

I do… Smack him in the face, harder than I meant to. He's
looking at me, lip bleeding. I want to apologise, say I didn't
mean to, that this isn't me. And he says:

'That's what I deserve.'

That makes me want to cry and I really really want to leave.
But that's not what I signed up for, so I get on with it.

Only later, back at home, tears fall. I was raised on a diet of Bollywood and romcoms so where the fuck is my happy ending?

ZAFAR. 'I have your previous statement, but I need you to tell me again.'

Ben is my new lawyer. He has dealt with LGBT asylum cases before and is putting my appeal together. I found him through the group and he is working for free.

Ben is good, he does everything well. This is our second meeting. I wonder if Ben is gay but I don't ask.

'I know it must be difficult.'

So I start again. The tears don't come this time. I try to stick to facts.

My father caught me with Haroon. I was locked in a room and beaten. He has links to the military and he would have killed me but I escaped. And there was a video.

I try not to picture Haroon's face, bloody and bruised. I don't want to think of him like that.

'Your partner was in the video?'

I question having to do this again, but I go on.

'Yes. He was beaten. And then they killed him.'

'How?'

What's the factual way of saying your father had his throat slit like a dog?

BILLY. Focus on the important things.

Throw myself into work, no time to think of anything else.

The first one in the office and the last one out.

This campaign for Pride is big and I'm all over it. One of the only advantages of being the son of immigrants is the work ethic you inherit. They didn't come here to fuck about – not like they do now – they came here to build something. My father built a chain of shops from nothing. He hustled.

And now I'm hustling.

It's gone seven and Fat Jason is leaving the office.

'Make sure you're not just all work.'

The promotion that's coming up, I can sense the competition.

'Don't worry. I always make time for the gym too.'

He nods and walks off.

It's good to keep people in their place.

ZAFAR. 'Excuse me, could you, I'm really sorry could you help me? I've…'

Doesn't even look in my direction. I get that from a lot of people here.

BILLY. Great, Amy's not coming. She's one of my best mates, but she continues to be flaky as fuck. More so now that she has a boyfriend. I've spent most of Pride with the work lot, and I just about got rid of them. But now thanks to Amy, it looks like I'm stuck in Soho with the plastics. We all used to work together years ago for Topshop (RIP), when Topshop and *Mean Girls* references were cool. Can only really tolerate them now when Amy is around. So what the fuck am I going to do?

Just gonna have to find some action. DRINK first!

ZAFAR. My phone's battery is dead. Stupid phone has a mind of its own. Was supposed to be meeting a couple of the guys from the group here, they came earlier. Now my phone isn't working and I can't find them. Knew this was a mistake. I didn't even really want to come.

This was Ben's idea.

BILLY. Too many people, can't settle on a target. Just need to get drunker, then my level of fussy won't mean a thing.

ZAFAR. Ben has been building my case. Said I should get statements from people in Pakistan, that the UK authorities should have taken pictures of my bruises.

'Having proof of your life here as a gay man would also make your case more credible.'

I tell him about the gay men's group.

'That's a good start, but you will need more. Is there anyone new in your life, a new partner?'

It's been over a year since Haroon died, but I'm still not ready for anything like that.

'Maybe even some evidence of you integrating into the gay community here?'

So here I am, integrating at Pride. My stupid phone doesn't even have a camera so I was hoping one of the guys could take some pictures here to prove to everyone I really am gay.

BILLY. 'Slow down, gurl, you're not gonna last.'

That piercing shrill is Da-ryl. Entertaining in small doses, very very small doses.

ZAFAR. Last text I got was that they were near Rupert Street bar, where the hell is Rupert Street and which bar?

BILLY. I keep drinking.

Jaime (just as annoying as Da-ryl) pipes up:

'Save yourself, got us all into that exclusive afterparty for British Airways, perk of marching in the parade.'

'Will we all have to look like big poofs too, in our trolley-dolly uniforms?'

'Someone collect her. I'm not looking after your drunk ass again.'

He is literally referring to an incident at Heaven ten years ago.

ZAFAR. I'm not leaving until I get something. I couldn't afford the Tube so I took two buses to get here. So I need to find them or find somewhere to charge my phone, I'm getting a bloody picture.

BILLY. 'I'll be fine, I can handle myself.'

'Isn't it against your religion to drink anyway.'

They all laugh.

'Fucking racist, Daryl.'

'I can't be racist, with the amount of Black DNA I've had in me I'm like eighty per cent black.'

'What's the other twenty per cent, gonorrhoea?'

ZAFAR. 'Excuse me, sir, could you…'

Probably wouldn't look at myself either. Everyone is in 3D technicolour, here I am sad and drab in black and white.

Still shocks me how free everyone seems, so at ease… Pride? Will I be like that? Occupy the same space with these people? The parties in university, hidden in cafés and bookshops, were nothing like this. We didn't dream to have pride, we just wanted to exist.

I turn a corner, stumble into an alleyway, two men having sex. I avert my gaze, but they don't stop, if anything they go harder and faster. I watch. I'm not the only one. How did I get here? How can this be the same world?

Panic rises in me, they have no fear…

And I'm no longer watching them, I'm being watched. I'm in the factory I manage for my father and it's late. It's just me and Haroon, before he has to get home to his family. And I'm greedy for him, all of him. I look up and it's my father staring back at me. I double-locked the door. I'm sure I did. He's looking at me with a look that no child should ever see in a parent's eyes. Pure hate.

I snap back to reality. My breath quickens like there isn't enough air. I need to get out of here. Find the group, be with people I know.

BILLY. Who the fuck does this guy look like?

'Just got back from a couple of weeks in Phuket.'

Hugh Grant? No. The other posh one like Hugh Grant, but younger.

Hugh Dancy?

ZAFAR. The crowd is thick in Soho. A face that doesn't look like Haroon, but shares something. The eyes, bright like the sun with a hint of sadness.

BILLY. Is that one, is Hugh Dancy a person?

'Don't cancel me, but with my tan I'm browner than you.'

He probably thinks I'm Italian, or more likely Persian.

'Stop. You're so... funny.'

ZAFAR. He's listening so intently.

BILLY. Dominic Cumberbatch!! That's it. No, that's two different ones, isn't it?

ZAFAR. App mereh madat kur suk-teh hein?

BILLY. 'What? You wanna try English, mate, I don't speak "pud pud ding ding" – '

I mean I can understand him, asking for help, but fuck him for assuming I can and in front of the white guy as well.

ZAFAR. You're Pakistani, no?

BILLY. British actually.

ZAFAR. I was asking if you could...

BILLY. I'm really flattered and everything, but you're not my type and I'm kind of in the middle of something.

ZAFAR. You've got it wrong, I was just asking...

BILLY. Look, I don't fuck Pakis, alright.

ZAFAR. Sorry to have distrubed you.

ZAFAR *walks off.*

BILLY. I don't feel bad 'cause, like, he needs to stay in his league, stepping to me. Don't think so.

I turn back to Josh O'Connor. That's who he looks like, the one from *The Crown*.

'Where were we?'

'It's sad that you can't speak your native tongue. I mean my boyfriend speaks Mandarin and Cantonese.'

BOYFRIEND!! For fuck's sake, boyfriend, like I've been listening to this fuckwit chat shit for like a lifetime and now he mentions a fucking boyfriend. I ain't got time for this.

He turns his back and walks off.

Better go and find the plastics, who knows where those poofs are now –

Fuck it, another drink first!

ACT TWO

ZAFAR. Sleep okay?

BILLY (*aside, to us*). He's in my bedroom holding a plate, and he's a Paki, like a proper one with an accent.

ZAFAR. I made breakfast, parathas, actually they're frozen ones from the shop. Eat.

BILLY (*aside, to us*). That's what the smell was. And now I'm really fucking confused.

Oh, umm. Sorry. Did we – ? You know – ? Fuck.

ZAFAR. You don't fuck Pakistanis, remember?

BILLY. Oh shit. I don't remember anything.

ZAFAR. Really?

BILLY. Really.

ZAFAR. You don't remember when you were an asshole and told me to go away?

BILLY. Yeah, actually I do remember that bit. Then not much. What are you doing here, in my bedroom?

ZAFAR. After eventually finding my friends (no thanks to you), I wasn't enjoying myself so I decided to leave. On my way to catch my bus you grabbed my arm. You were outside another bar, drunk, with these two dodgy guys. Asking me to help you. You spoke in Urdu so they wouldn't understand.

BILLY. Fuck. I kind of remember the guys… they were full-on. And you helped me, right?

ZAFAR. Told them, 'What the hell you doing with my friend? I've been looking for him everywhere.' And I just took you. I barely had money for the bus so we had to go to a cash machine which was a nightmare. You really should never sing. Then we got a taxi here… By the way, I used your change to get us breakfast… you only have powders in your cupboards.

BILLY. That's fine. And you stayed?

ZAFAR. I didn't know how to get back to Hounslow from here plus you wouldn't let me leave. You told me the whole storyline to *Kuch Kuch Hota Hai* twice. And then fell asleep.

BILLY. Why? I've not seen that in ages, I stopped watching Bollywood as a kid.

ZAFAR. When you discovered gay porn.

BILLY. What? Fuck.

ZAFAR. You told me that yesterday.

BILLY. Did I?

ZAFAR. By the way, you snore. So I slept on the couch.

BILLY. Thank you.

ZAFAR. Don't worry about it. I'm sure you'd do the same for me.

BILLY. Yeah. (*Aside, to us.*) Now I feel like a right prick.

ZAFAR. Eat.

They eat.

BILLY. You're the first one who's ever made me breakfast. Normally just want them to fuck off.

ZAFAR. Sorry. I can leave?

BILLY. I didn't mean that. Just, this is sweet. Thank you, you've been really kind.

My mum used to make these all the time. Carbs, I love it.

ZAFAR. I can tell.

BILLY. So how long have you been here? In the country.

ZAFAR. About a year.

BILLY. You have family here?

ZAFAR. No.

BILLY. Lucky you. I've got too much family. Don't you miss it?

ZAFAR. Pakistan? Of course it's home. Have you ever been?

BILLY. Only as a kid, stopped going by the time I was sixteen. Hated giving up my holidays, just wanted to hang out with my mates.

ZAFAR. Where in Pakistan are you from?

BILLY. Haven't been asked that in a while.

ZAFAR. You don't have to answer.

BILLY. It's cool. My family are mainly in Lahore.

ZAFAR. I'm from a village not too far.

BILLY. I don't know much about the rest of the place.

ZAFAR. Well, I went to the university in Lahore. Beautiful city.

BILLY. Really? What did you study?

ZAFAR. Business. I wanted to do something more creative, but you know how it is…

BILLY. Yep. I did Business and Management, and disappointed my parents by working in fashion.

ZAFAR. Me too! Not the disappointing part, well, not in that way at least.

I was in charge of my father's textile factory. My favourite was always helping to choose the prints. These designs that have been passed down through generations, this fabric steeped in the history of the region, every piece telling a story. I would often think about the secret history woven into that fabric. The legacy of the queers who came before us. What they were trying to communicate.

BILLY. I mainly sell crop-tops to teenagers.

ZAFAR. I mean even that tells a story. No? The way you choose to dress is important. (*Aside, to us.*) I suddenly become super-conscious of what I'm wearing.

BILLY. Yeah, do you know any Western designers?

ZAFAR. Of course. I love Alexander McQueen,

BILLY. Really? He is one of my all-time favourites. A genius.

ZAFAR. Each piece was like a work of art.

BILLY. Yeah the detail, the originality.

ZAFAR. His legacy.

BILLY. I went like four times to his exhibition at the V&A, amazing!

ZAFAR. You're so lucky... I'd google it, wishing I could get to New York or London to see it.

BILLY. Have you been to the V&A? Fascinating.

ZAFAR. No. I haven't really seen much of London. I'd like to do all the touristy things.

BILLY. Why don't you then?

ZAFAR. ...No time.

BILLY. Always the way when you live in a city. Never thought someone from back home would be into McQueen.

ZAFAR. Why not?

BILLY. Assumed it was all kurtas and tank tops?

ZAFAR. Never seen a Pakistani drama, it's all glamour now.

BILLY. I can quite proudly say I've never have.

ZAFAR. Right. My next mission is to get you into them.

BILLY. I don't think so.

ZAFAR. Honestly, they're so good, they import them all over the world.

BILLY. I mean it's nice to talk about Paki stuff, but I'm not watching that shit.

ZAFAR. Maybe stop calling it 'Paki stuff'.

BILLY. I don't mean it in a bad way.

ZAFAR. So there is a good way to use it?

BILLY. Okay. My point was: this is nice. I don't really have that many Pakistani people in my life.

ZAFAR. Your family?

BILLY. Moved to the other side of London for a reason.

ZAFAR. You don't visit?

BILLY. Became an exercise in self-harm. So I stopped. Mum's always asking to see me, but fuck going home and having to deal with that.

ZAFAR. So they know.

BILLY. Yes. Told them after my second year of uni. They hoped it was a phase or that praying would fix it. Now they're happy to tolerate me if I just don't do or say anything that reminds them I'm gay.

And yours?

ZAFAR. I mean… Actually, that's a story for another time. I had to leave Pakistan because I'm gay.

BILLY. That's why I don't bother. It's the same with the Pakis here. Fucking backwards. What I hate about it: the culture, the people always in your business, the religion…

ZAFAR. It's not the religion – some of the people maybe? But homophobia exists everywhere, even here with English people.

BILLY. Not in the same way.

ZAFAR. The British are the ones who made it illegal in Pakistan.

BILLY. That was years ago now. I mean, even India's managed to get over it. But fucking Pakis.

ZAFAR. That word again. We're both Pakistani and we don't think like that. Pakistan is a big country, Islam is a big religion. If five per cent of people are gay then that means there are a hundred million gay Muslims. People who would think differently, who would interpret those verses in the Quran differently.

BILLY. Not when they're all too afraid to show themselves.

ZAFAR. Maybe you're right. All I know is that Islam has brought me more peace than pain.

BILLY. I mean, I still pray, like before I go into an important meeting or something. Old habit. Stupid.

ZAFAR. If it brings you peace you don't need to question it.

BILLY. True.

ZAFAR. I should go.

BILLY. I didn't mean to upset you.

ZAFAR. You haven't.

BILLY. Then stay a bit longer. If you can.

ZAFAR. I mean…

BILLY. I'll even watch a Pakistani drama.

ZAFAR. Well, how can I say no then?

(*Aside, to us.*) We end up watching three episodes of *Humsafar* on Netflix.

Sitting here watching TV. Something I haven't felt in a long time. Normal.

When I leave he suggests we swap numbers.

BILLY. I need to take you out or something to say a proper thank-you.

ZAFAR. You don't have to do that.

BILLY. Do one of those tourist things?

ZAFAR. Sounds good. I better go. Kudahfiz, Bilal.

BILLY. You know you've been doing that all day… My name's – I actually prefer Billy.

ZAFAR. Billy? Like cat in Urdu.

BILLY. Yeah…

ZAFAR. As you wish. Bye… Billy.

ZAFAR *leaves*.

BILLY. Bilal… the way he says it. Reminds me of how my parents would say it.

That evening I think about them a lot. My family, all of them, the whole tribe…

Last time I saw them was over a year ago. The conversation never got beyond polite chit-chat. Mum tells me about a cousin that had a baby and adds, 'I always pray you'll have a proper family and kids.'

I know what she means by 'proper'. Resist the urge to say I will when I find the right guy. I just leave early, promise to visit again soon, but I know I won't.

I'm tolerated, that should be enough, right?

ZAFAR (*to* BILLY). Sorry, sorry. You got my text?

BILLY. You're thirty minutes late and I had to just stand here, like an idiot.

ZAFAR. I know. So sorry, the buses.

BILLY. You could have just got the Tube.

ZAFAR. The bus is normally reliable.

BILLY. Forget it. Let's just walk along the river.

ZAFAR. Sure.

BILLY. I might get myself a gin and tonic from over there, do you want one?

ZAFAR. I don't drink.

BILLY. –

ZAFAR. Please, you go ahead, it's fine.

BILLY. No, don't worry then.

They walk.

ZAFAR. So many people.

BILLY. Yeah.

ZAFAR. Interesting to see London like this, like a tourist.

BILLY *pulls out his phone and opens Grindr.*

It's beautiful, how the old just sits with the new.

BILLY. Sorry, you don't mind, do you? Just checking the local talent.

ZAFAR. That's fine.

BILLY *(aside, to us).* Good, need him to know this isn't a date.

ZAFAR. Anyone interesting?

BILLY. Same old, same old.

They walk in silence.

ZAFAR. Is everything okay?

BILLY. Yeah, why?

ZAFAR. Thank you for arranging this, I don't know many people in London. It can be lonely, so this is super-kind.

BILLY *puts his phone away.*

BILLY. I'm just a bit tired, work has been majorly stressful.

ZAFAR. Again I'm sorry to add to that stress.

BILLY. You've already apologised enough.

ZAFAR. Come on, tell me – what's stressing you out?

BILLY. Nothing.

ZAFAR. What are friends for?

BILLY. Okay. I had an interview today for a promotion.

ZAFAR. That's great news.

BILLY. Yeah. But I just really want it. I mean I've basically been doing the job for the last six months with no extra pay. Got a feeling they're going to give it to Fat Jason.

ZAFAR. What makes you think that?

BILLY. I don't know, just a hunch.

ZAFAR. Sounds like you just need to trust how great you are. Inshallah you'll get it.

BILLY. Let's hope they think so too.

ZAFAR. They'd be fools not to pick you. From the sounds of it they need you more than you need them. Remember your worth.

BILLY. Yeah. You're right. What do you do for work, here in London?

ZAFAR. Umm. Just between things... Know what really amazes me about England? No one actually speaks English. 'Innit bruv?' 'That's banging' – I can just about understand them now.

BILLY. You almost sound like a native.

ZAFAR. I'm not sure that's a compliment. 'Leng' – what's that one?

BILLY. Someone called you leng?

ZAFAR. A boy at the bus stop shouted it at a girl and she just kissed her teeth and walked off.

BILLY. It's an upgrade from peng... like someone who's hot, looks good.

ZAFAR. Learn something new every day, innit bredrin.

They laugh.

BILLY (*aside, to us*). We end up walking all the way to The Shard and back. I mean he's a nice guy, a bit odd. He texts a day later and suggests a walk around Hyde Park. I don't respond straight away, but then I realise I don't have any weekend plans again.

ZAFAR. Race you to the lamp post.

They both run. ZAFAR *wins.*

Beat you, Mr Fitness.

BILLY. I'm still sore from the gym yesterday and you had a head start.

ZAFAR. Sounds like excuses to me.

BILLY. Next time we're gonna do something that involves sitting and just watching.

ZAFAR. Okay. Loser. Watched any more *Humsafar*?

BILLY. Finished it.

ZAFAR. You're joking.

BILLY. No.

ZAFAR. Wow. That was quick.

BILLY. I have a tendency to binge-watch, okay?

ZAFAR. So it's safe to say you're into Pakistani dramas then?

BILLY. I've started *Zindagi Gulzar Hai*.

ZAFAR. Really? So you've got a thing for Fawad Khan? Maybe Pakistanis aren't so bad after all.

BILLY. I mean, it's purely because he's a very charismatic leading man. That stuff is like crack, now I know why my mother never leaves the TV.

ZAFAR. My mum, she used to… Never mind.

BILLY. Go on.

ZAFAR. Not that interesting.

BILLY. So what have you been up to today?

ZAFAR. Nothing much.

BILLY. Not working?

ZAFAR. No.

BILLY. Still don't even know what you do?

ZAFAR. I said… no? In between things.

BILLY. That's not really an answer. You know you're always
    happier when it's me talking.

ZAFAR. Honestly. Nothing to tell.

BILLY. Fine.

ZAFAR. No that's the truth. I don't do anything. That's what
    I do all day.

    Actually that's not entirely true. Today was Wednesday so
    I got to go and sign in, like I do every week to prove I haven't
    run off. Like I have somewhere to run to.

BILLY. Are you illegal?

ZAFAR. I'm an asylum seeker.

BILLY. So you're allowed to be here?

ZAFAR. For the moment. I'm seeking protection in the UK,
    have a case in the system. I couldn't stay in Pakistan.

BILLY. Because you're gay? You said that when you were at
    mine.

ZAFAR. Yes. My life was in danger, because…

BILLY. You don't have to.

ZAFAR. It's okay, it's not my first time. My father, he found out
    and then he tried to kill me.

BILLY. Your father?

ZAFAR. He's ex-army. He ordered other men to murder my
    partner, Haroon.

    And because of him everyone knows about me, so if I ever
    go back and he doesn't finish me off they'll just throw me
    in jail.

BILLY. Fuck. That's… I'm so sorry.

ZAFAR. So now you know.

BILLY. And you escaped?

ZAFAR. Used my brother's passport, he had a visa from when he came here for a conference, and got here on a flight pretending to be him.

BILLY. I can't... I don't even... I'm so sorry.

ZAFAR. You have nothing to be sorry about.

BILLY. Here I am worried about my stuff... And in comparison...

ZAFAR. It's all relative.

BILLY. Fuck. I'm glad you're here now and safe.

ZAFAR. For now.

BILLY. What?

ZAFAR. They could send me back.

BILLY. To Pakistan?

ZAFAR. Or who knows, even Rwanda.

BILLY. They wouldn't do that?

ZAFAR. The Home Office has already rejected me once, I am appealing at the moment.

BILLY. But you'll be fine... You're in Britain now. They wouldn't send a gay person back, to be harmed.

ZAFAR. I'm not in your Britain. I'm in another Britain. I spend every hour worrying if I will be allowed to stay. David from my peer support group, he was from Uganda. He had to run because he was being blackmailed by a police officer and had been attacked. He was sent back, without anyone knowing, put on a flight and no one has heard from him since.

BILLY. Some people lie. I'm not saying him or you, but some people pretend to be gay just to play the system. So they have to be careful.

ZAFAR. And who knows what desperation led them to do that...? It takes a lot to say those words if you are gay, let alone if you're not.

BILLY. I didn't mean it like that.

Beat.

I won't let that happen to you. I promise.

ZAFAR. Thank you, Bilal. Billy. I meant Billy.

BILLY. Don't worry about it. Just call me Bilal if you like.

ZAFAR. Don't start treating me differently.

BILLY. I like you saying it, the proper way.

ZAFAR. I don't want pity.

BILLY. Trust me, you won't get any from me.

ZAFAR. That day I was at yours, was the first time in a long time I was just Zafar, normal Zafar. I liked it.

BILLY. And you still are.

Let's get something to eat?

ZAFAR. I can't, I barely have money for the bus.

BILLY. My treat. I still owe you a thank-you for saving me.

ZAFAR. No you don't.

BILLY. You made me parathas.

ZAFAR. Well, I defrosted them.

BILLY. That's more than enough.

ZAFAR. Okay.

(*Aside, to us.*) And it's his treat every time we meet after that too. So I try to eat from home, only have a tea so he doesn't have to pay too much.

BILLY. You can't just sit there and watch me eat, so a big popcorn to share.

ZAFAR. If the government ever allows me to work I will pay you back for this.

BILLY. What, some popcorn? Don't worry about it. Still no news?

ZAFAR. About my appeal? No... you will get bored of asking that question. Could take ages. One person in my group has been waiting five years.

BILLY. Fucking hell.

ZAFAR. I promise any news I'll let you know.

BILLY. Okay. Also brought you a few bits of clothes. I don't need them and they'd look good on you.

ZAFAR. You really didn't have to.

BILLY. It was nothing.

ZAFAR. Thank you. It'll be nice to wear something else for a change.

BILLY. Trailers are starting.

ZAFAR *watches him*.

What?

ZAFAR. Nothing.

(*Aside, to us.*) We end up watching loads of movies, usually at his place. Mine isn't an option, I'm not allowed visitors.

It feels nice to know I have a friend. I mean, the guys from the support group are friends too, but this, this is different.

BILLY. Ta-dah.

ZAFAR. This is a beach?

BILLY. Yes... there's the sea.

ZAFAR. All the beaches I know have sand.

BILLY. It's a pebble beach.

ZAFAR. That's a thing?

BILLY. Welcome to Brighton.

ZAFAR. At least it's not Hounslow. You have no idea how good it feels just to leave the accommodation. This is a beautiful surprise.

BILLY. Every gay needs to visit Brighton at least once. Went to uni here. Have many happy memories of getting drunk and pulling random guys on the dance floor of Club Revenge.

ZAFAR. That's a cool name for a club. Revenge!

BILLY. Really?

ZAFAR. Very dramatic.

BILLY. It all was when you're that age.

ZAFAR. So there were many?

BILLY. You asking for my body count?

ZAFAR. Your what?

BILLY. Body count. How many guys I've been with.

ZAFAR. No! I wasn't. But, I mean, if you want to share…

BILLY. Not really.

ZAFAR. You've just never talked about anyone.

BILLY. No one to talk about.

ZAFAR. What do you mean?

BILLY. Exactly that.

ZAFAR. But look at you, you must have your pick of the bunch.

BILLY. Sex is easy, but none of them stick.

ZAFAR. Well, they're stupid.

BILLY. Maybe… or maybe it's me.

ZAFAR. Now you're being stupid.

BILLY. Am I? When I first came out, I thought my Prince Charming was just around the corner. But being Asian and fat like I was then means you're bottom of the pile.

ZAFAR. You shouldn't think like that.

BILLY. It's not me, it's just the way it is. I remember the first guy I ever had sex with said I didn't smell the same as other Pakistanis. I took it as a compliment.

I was picked on at school for being a fat brown poof and ironically it was the same with the gays. I've done everything I can to fit the mould, and still nothing.

ZAFAR. Maybe it's just the type of guys you go for?

BILLY. You can't help your preferences.

ZAFAR. Sounds like something a white man would say.

BILLY. Now you're calling me a coconut. Well, we can't all be as lucky as you.

ZAFAR. Lucky? I mean, I could think of other words.

BILLY. Sorry, I meant, to have had that, to have found that with someone.

ZAFAR. Haroon was married. It was far from a perfect situation, but yeah even in Pakistan sex is easy, love not so much. So you hold on to what you find.

Silence.

I have a surprise.

ZAFAR *pulls out a piece of embroidery from his bag.*

BILLY. What?

ZAFAR. Now you need to close your eyes.

BILLY *does as he's told.*

Ta-dah.

BILLY. Did you make this?

ZAFAR. Yes. I had to beg, borrow and steal the kit and thread, usually it's silk.

BILLY. It's beautiful.

ZAFAR. It's phulkari, passed down through generations of Punjabi women. Expressing their emotions through the designs, their hopes and fears as they went to start new lives. It's not as common now.

BILLY. I didn't know you were so talented.

ZAFAR. My mum taught me when I was little. Maybe without a daughter I was the next best thing. I stopped when I got older. But now I have the time and I don't have to worry what my dad would think.

BILLY. Thank you.

ZAFAR. Pleasure. You will meet someone inshallah.

BILLY. Inshallah. Food?

ZAFAR. And then Club Revenge!

Naff song plays.

So this is it?

BILLY. Yeah.

ZAFAR. You drank a lot right?

BILLY. Yeah.

Beat.

Shall we leave?

ZAFAR. Yeah.

(*Aside, to us.*) We decided to stick to movies and food after that. I find it hard to believe Bilal has never found that someone. What if that someone was me?

BILLY. Weekend done. Monday morning. Back to the grind and the shit begins. I didn't get the fucking promotion. Fuck that. About, I don't have enough experience... I'm doing the job!! Have been for the last six months.

Need to call Zafar. He's good with this. Genuinely listens, cares.

He rings.

He's not answering.

ZAFAR. I'm still in bed. Missed call, Bilal.

I think of him while I lie here. Wearing one of the jumpers he gave me. Smells of him. Smells nice. There could be a different life for me here, one not on my own. With him. A relationship would be proof for my asylum case. That would help. Integrated. Happy.

I have to stop this, he doesn't even fuck Pakistanis, remember? To be that confused. Sometimes I'm the one who ends up feeling sorry for him. I have to deal with being Pakistani, but he has to deal with being British and Pakistani.

And then like always I think about Haroon.

BILLY. Walking out the building, try to call Zafar again when Fat Jason stops me in the corridor… He's the last person I want to speak to.

'I heard you didn't get the promotion.'

Great, he's here to gloat.

'You should have got it, you were the best person.'

That was nice of him, I mean, he didn't have to say that. Actually, why am I such a cunt to him again?

ZAFAR. Another call from Bilal. But I can't.

It is his birthday today. Haroon.

Not sure if you can hear me but happy birthday.

How do I stop loving you?

And I already know the answer. I don't want to stop.

BILLY. I've been working with Fat Jason – sorry – I mean Jason for ages and I don't know anything about him. So us having lunch is a bit awkward at first, but then we just get chatting away.

Turns out he didn't even apply for the promotion. He knows the guy who got it.

'They just employed another white man to join the all-white management team.'

I don't know what to say to that. Makes me think about it in a way I hadn't before, or hadn't wanted to.

Nah, it can't be that, can it?

Then he asks me if I celebrate Eid.

'Sometimes, why?'

'It's on Tuesday.'

I totally forgot. He knows, 'cause Jason's partner is… Muslim! Indian Muslim. And now I have so many questions.

He's a barrister, they met at uni. Been together since then… His parents know he's gay and they know about Jason. At first they were having none of it but now Jason's one of the family. He'll be there for Eid.

Slightly jealous of people who find the one so easily and even more jealous of brown boys who can bring them home to their parents.

He asks me again what my Eid plans are.

'I'll probably just end up spending it with Zafar. He's a mate, but I haven't known him for ages, but he's becoming like a good mate, we hang out loads and he comes over to mine a lot… But that's because his place is depressing and he's not allowed people over.'

Jason gives me a look like: 'Oh yeah!'

'No, it's not like that, he's not my type, he's an asylum seeker.' Why did I say the last bit? Feels like I said something bad.

Jason doesn't register, he's telling me his other half does something to do with that. I'm only half listening again, and I can't concentrate for the rest of the day. He's not just an asylum seeker, he's Zafar. Why did I say that?

I mean, he's not my type but he's not ugly. Naturally slim, eyes that radiate goodness, a face that the more you look at the more you find. And a really banging personality…

He'd make anyone a great boyfriend.

(*To* ZAFAR.) You were right. Know my worth. If that shit company can't see how much I bring then I just need to go someplace where they will.

ZAFAR. Good.

BILLY. You're quiet today.

ZAFAR. Just tired.

BILLY. Everything okay? Is it your appeal?

ZAFAR. No. Everything's okay.

BILLY. I was worried, when I couldn't get through yesterday I thought something happened. You should let me get you a new phone.

ZAFAR. It wasn't the phone, I just didn't feel like talking.

BILLY. Oh. Right.

ZAFAR. Not just with you. With anyone. I didn't even go to the support group yesterday.

BILLY. You don't need to talk, we can just sit. But you're okay?

Beat.

Zafar?

ZAFAR. It's stupid.

BILLY. You can tell me.

ZAFAR. It was his birthday yesterday. Haroon's.

BILLY. Right.

ZAFAR. See, I told you.

BILLY. It's not stupid. How old would he have been?

ZAFAR. Thirty-three.

BILLY. That's young.

ZAFAR. Too young.

BILLY. Did you do anything? To mark it?

ZAFAR. No.

BILLY. I know it's not the same but after my nani died, on her birthday, we would all get together and share memories about her. My favourite was how she always called a jacket potato a Jackie potato, and would wear a cardigan come rain or shine. I swear even to bed.

Tell me about him.

ZAFAR. It wasn't actually really his real birthday. No one in his family recorded that properly, so he didn't know the day he was born. When we were kids I made yesterday his birthday and made sure we'd celebrate it every year just the two of us. Even when I went to university I made sure I was back to be with him, and every year I'd put a candle in a doughnut for him.

BILLY. A doughnut?

ZAFAR. The only thing I had in the house was a doughnut, no cake, he loved it. First time he'd had one. It became our tradition every year. A doughnut with a candle in it.

BILLY. I wish I could have met him.

ZAFAR. You would have liked him. He had such a beautiful nature and he was pretty hot.

BILLY. Wait there.

BILLY *goes off and quickly returns with a candle in a protein bar.*

I didn't have a doughnut.

ZAFAR. It's perfect.

BILLY. Make a wish.

ZAFAR *blows out the candle.*

(*Aside, to us.*) I've managed to, last minute, book Tuesday off. Told the boss it was a religious holiday and he just looked at me funny. But fuck him, me and Zafar are gonna spend the day together because it's Eid. So the plan is that I'll come to Hounslow for lunch, the food's better (one good thing about it being Asian Central), then back to mine for a movie marathon.

When I arrive he makes me wait outside. He's not allowed visitors in his accommodation, but I also don't think he wanted me to see where he lives. I mean I wouldn't care.

ZAFAR. Vah vah app bilqul hero lagreh hai. [You look like a star.]

BILLY. App vee both acha lega teh hai? [You also look good.] Don't laugh, my Urdu is bad.

ZAFAR. It's not, it's just the London accent. But seriously you look proper leng. Never seen you wear desi clothes before.

BILLY. Thanks. It's Jason's boyfriend's, I don't own one.

ZAFAR. The one you call Fat Jason.

BILLY. Yeah, we shouldn't call him that any more.

ZAFAR. I never called him that.

BILLY. He's alright it turns out.

They hug for a fraction too long.

ZAFAR. His muscles clench under the cotton of his kameez.

BILLY. He smells good. Like really good.

ZAFAR *breaks the hug.*

After a lunch that consisted of way too much food, we're back at my place. I whack on an old Bollywood movie.

ZAFAR. Maybe you should try watching one from this decade.

BILLY. I only like the classics, they're the best.

ZAFAR. I mean, some of the new ones are really good, if you ignore all the Islamophobia.

BILLY *looks at* ZAFAR.

What?

BILLY. Nothing.

(*Aside, to us.*) I reach for some crisps on the table, and in that moment make a decision.

ZAFAR. His arm doesn't go back to where it was.

BILLY. Hand shaking as I move it closer to him.

ZAFAR. His arm is over my shoulders.

BILLY. My heart beats faster.

ZAFAR. My breath quickens.

BILLY. I look at him.

ZAFAR. He looks at me.

BILLY *and* ZAFAR. Our eyes lock.

BILLY (*to* ZAFAR). Are you okay?

ZAFAR. I nod, not sure what else to do.

BILLY. Lips millimetres away.

ZAFAR. I want to.

BILLY. I want to.

ZAFAR. His lips pressed up against mine. And a stupid thought enters my brain. My last kiss was with him, with Haroon.

(*To* BILLY.) Don't come near me.

BILLY. I was just –

ZAFAR. Don't. How desperate do you think I am? I would never. Will never. Understand –

BILLY. Desperate? Fuck off. Look at you, and look at me… Just fucking LEAVE.

ZAFAR *leaves*.

Immediately, I know I shouldn't have said that.

What is so fucking wrong with me? I'm thirty-one and I've never been in a relationship. People always say it'll happen when you're not looking for it, it'll take you by surprise. And here I am still waiting. I thought this might be different, he's literally the opposite of what I should go for and not even he wants me.

ZAFAR. It's the day after Eid… Have to be at the centre to sign in at nine. Too tired to get out of bed, didn't sleep. Everything is such a mess and more bad stuff just keeps getting added.

Bilal was right, should be lucky someone like him was interested in me… look how damaged I am, how much baggage I bring. I want to wallow here all day, but I can't miss this appointment to sign in, so I force myself out of bed.

BILLY. I feel worse, next morning. Have no excuse. Zafar has been through so much, he doesn't need this. He's a good person and I'm… well, I'm not.

I send a message saying – 'I'm sorry.'

I arrive at work and nothing.

Lunchtime, nothing.

Gym, nothing.

Maybe he just needs time?

Don't hear from him the day after either. Send him another text. Nothing.

When I call, straight to voicemail.

Now I'm worried. Something's not right.

ZAFAR. Bus is late so I'm now running up the stairs to the entrance of the sign-in office… I'm signing in as normal when someone asks me to follow them.

They have good news.

I follow and when I enter the side room I don't notice them at first.

'Zafar Mahmood?'

'Yes.'

They circle me...

'You do not have to say anything. But, it may harm your defence...'

The cold metal of the handcuffs clamp my wrists.

'What are you doing, why are you arresting me?'

'You're illegal in this country and you've overstayed.'

'But I have an appeal in process – '

They don't care, they put me in the back of a van.

BILLY. Travel down to his temporary accommodation. No one's seen him. Then a man who's walking out the building with his daughter says he heard he got taken away.

'What? Taken where and by who?'

ZAFAR. I'd heard about this place in the group, but I wasn't ready for this hell. It should just be called a prison.

It's filthy, the toilets overflowing, the food awful. Defecating in a toilet full of other people's shit.

Five o'clock I'm finally given a chance to speak to my lawyer. Ben's away on holiday this week, but someone else will get back to me.

My stupid phone is dead, it's not switching on, so I can't call anyone.

Next day someone else from the firm tells me:

'The Home Office says they can't trace your appeal documents, so we're sending them again and then we'll work on getting you released.'

They can't tell me when? Or how the Home Office could misplace all my papers.

Barely eat or sleep, can't bring myself to.

Just sit here thinking of the worst and then it happens.

BILLY. Have to find him? I don't have a clue where to start. Then I remember Jason saying his partner worked in this stuff.

(*On the phone.*) It's Zafar, we had a fight, but he's disappeared. Not heard from him since Eid. I went to his accommodation and someone said the Home Office took him. Can you please help me find him?

Jason says he'll speak to his boyfriend, Javid, turns out he's a lawyer. I text him all Zafar's details, name, age, where he was staying. Javid finds out Zafar has been removed to Colnbrook detention centre.

ZAFAR. 'You will be sent back to Pakistan tomorrow afternoon.'

'Just kill me here, please, I beg you, I would prefer that.'

The guard doesn't respond.

It's Friday afternoon, so the law firm can't do anything.

'Please, God, please.' I switch on my phone…

One per cent battery!!

Types out a text.

I hit send and my battery dies.

BILLY (*receives text*). 'Help me. They're sending me to Lahore tomorrow afternoon.'

ZAFAR. Two men force me into the back of a car. I'm being driven to the airport.

BILLY. In the back of an Uber heading to Heathrow. Pat my pocket to make sure my passport is still there.

Javid put me in touch with Lesbians and Gays Support the Migrants.

They worked out that Zafar must be on the two o'clock British Airways flight out of Heathrow. BA is the only airline that deports people to Pakistan and this is the only afternoon flight to Lahore. We tried a Twitter storm, get BA enough bad press and they'd remove him from the flight. Seventy likes... seventy fucking likes was all we got.

Work wouldn't let me use their account, it's a bit too political for them apparently. So much for supporting the queer community. The bastards.

ZAFAR. My legs go. They hoist me up from my armpits and force me to walk down the aisle to the back of the plane. I think of the others who have taken these very same steps. I should kick and scream, but I don't have the energy.

BILLY. Run through all the checks and make it to the plane as they're doing the final boarding.

ZAFAR. The last people board the plane, each one a grain of sand in an hourglass.

I close my eyes. Think of something else, think of something else.

BILLY. I'm in my seat and was instructed by Lesbians and Gays Support the Migrants to only get up and refuse to sit back down when the seat-belt sign goes on.

What if we've got it wrong? What if he's not on this flight? Zafar, please be on this flight. Please be on this flight.

ZAFAR. Never got to say goodbye. Haroon, and now Bilal.

Thank you, Bilal. Thank you for everything.

And, Haroon, I'll be with you soon.

BILLY. I look around the flight again, it dawns on me, it's full of Pakistanis. Obviously it's a flight to Lahore. But I'm gonna have to get up in front of all these people.

Fuck. The seat-belt light is on.

ZAFAR. The seat-belt light flashes. I have an impulse to get up and run. But the guards are sitting beside me.

BILLY. I can't do this, I can't do this… but I have to.

He stands.

'Can you sit back down please, sir.' It's an air steward,
blatantly gay, in the BA uniform I last saw at Pride. 'Sir, the
seat-belt light is on.'

I start pacing the aisle.

'You need to sit down, otherwise we can't take off.'

People are looking.

'I will not sit down! There is an asylum seeker on this plane.
His name is Zafar Mahmood and he is being forcibly
removed and sent to his death in Pakistan. I will not allow
this plane to take off until he is safely off this flight.'

And I keep repeating that.

'There is an asylum seeker on this plane. His name is Zafar
Mahmood and he is being forcibly removed and sent to his
death. There is an asylum seeker on this plane. His name is
Zafar Mahmood and he is being forcibly removed and sent to
his death…'

BILLY *keeps on repeating his demands as* ZAFAR *speaks.*

ZAFAR. There is a commotion, further up ahead. This is my
chance? I get up, I'm pushed back down.

'I just want to look.'

Shouts erupt from passengers asking what is going on.

BILLY. I feel a hand on my shoulder. It's an air steward.

He jerks off the hand.

'Don't fucking touch me!… There is an asylum seeker on
this plane. His name is Zafar Mahmood and he is being
forcibly removed and sent to his death.'

'They don't just kill people in Pakistan, you know, he must
have done something.'

'He hasn't done anything... He's a gay man like me, he has every right to live.'

'Faggots!'

We hear the reactions of people on the plane throughout this section: 'Faggots!' 'Gandu!' 'Just let them off!' 'You're delaying everyone!'

'Oww... fuck.'

Something hard smacks the back of my head. Fucking stings.

And I go back to repeating my demands.

'There is an asylum seeker on this plane. His name is Zafar Mahmood and he is being forcibly removed. There / is an asylum seeker on this plane...

WOMAN (*voice-over*). There is an asylum seeker on this plane. His name is Zafar Mahmood, he is being forcibly removed.

The woman's voice carries on throughout the following.

BILLY. Next to me is a woman old enough to be my mum. Repeating my demands with me. I want to fucking hug her so bad.

ZAFAR. The chatter of people is loud.

The guards look at each other, agitated.

BILLY. Some people have got their phones out filming. A couple of teenage girls stand in support. While others mutter in disgust.

A man gets up and he's built like a bull.

'You need to sit back down, bro, or I'll make you sit back down.'

ZAFAR. The people are getting out of their seats. My name in other passengers' mouths.

'Yes. Yes. I'm Zafar Mahmood!'

BILLY. The bull is in my face, the steward intercedes.

'Sir, you're not helping, we've got this in hand.'

ZAFAR. The guard is telling me to shut up. But I don't.

'I'm Zafar Mahmood!'

BILLY. 'Fucking stone them all.'

The bull is getting more irate, he looks like he's going to punch the steward.

It's fucking chaos. As people argue and shout. The air steward says he needs to speak to the pilot.

ZAFAR. The guard left behind is on his mobile.

'He's on the plane, I'm not losing my bonus over this.'

BILLY. The rest of the cabin crew are trying to calm things down.

ZAFAR. He turns to his colleague.

'We've been fucking instructed to remove him from the flight.'

BILLY. 'There are children on this plane, they don't need to hear about your sort.'

'There is a GAY asylum seeker on this plane his name is Zafar Mahmood – '

ZAFAR. I'm lifted up and they're walking up the aisle.

BILLY. I see him. Zafar.

ZAFAR. I see him. Bilal?

BILLY. He's being led from the back of the plane, his hands are bound with a yellow plastic tie.

ZAFAR. He's smiling at me so broadly. I question my grip on reality. And before I'm aware I'm off the plane.

BILLY. The gay air steward approaches me.

'The captain agrees it's no longer safe with him on the plane. He's been removed from the flight.'

And with that he takes me to the door and I think I hear him whisper: 'Well done.'

He's fucking safe… for now.

Epilogue

ZAFAR. The train from London has just pulled in, I spot him in the distance. He cuts a fine figure as always, I resist the urge to run towards him, but as he draws closer I can't help myself.

ZAFAR *runs and hugs* BILAL.

You're famous. All over social media and the news.

BILAL. Stop it.

ZAFAR. You're a hero.

BILAL. Depends who you ask.

ZAFAR. According to the Quran you are: whoever saves a life, it will be as if they saved all of humanity.

BILAL. If only everyone focused on the important bits.

ZAFAR. Journey okay?

BILAL. Yeah. See, Portsmouth's not so far.

ZAFAR. I never thought I'd miss Hounslow so much.

BILAL. You not settling in?

ZAFAR. I'm fine, it's fine. The actual accommodation is a bit better, it's just starting again somewhere new.

BILAL. Ridiculous how quickly they just gave your room away.

ZAFAR. Thank you for coming, thank you for everything.

BILAL. You don't have to thank me.

ZAFAR. You could go to jail.

BILAL. My lawyer is saying it's ninety per cent likely the charges will be dropped.

ZAFAR. My lawyer is saying all the attention will work in my favour, when they hear my appeal. But still no date… Still waiting.

BILAL. After all that and nothing?

ZAFAR. I'm a high-profile figure now, there is no way they can tell me I'm not homosexual and force me back to Pakistan. I'll be fine. Don't worry. How many planes are you going to stop for me?

BILAL. As many as I need to.

ZAFAR. Wow, very Bollywood.

BILAL. If it was Bollywood there would be a big song-and-dance number too.

ZAFAR. And there'd be a kiss.

BILAL. They don't kiss in Bollywood films.

ZAFAR. If you had ever watched a new Bollywood film you'd know they do now.

Come here I'll show you.

ZAFAR *kisses* BILAL. *A shift. The actors become themselves.*

ACTOR ONE (ZAFAR). I don't know how I feel about this?

ACTOR TWO (BILAL). What?

ACTOR ONE. This ending.

ACTOR TWO. It's a happy ending.

ACTOR ONE. We're perpetuating a myth. How many people have a Bilal? How many people get pulled off a flight once they're on?

ACTOR TWO. Some do.

ACTOR ONE. Not enough. Not enough for them to think this is normal.

ACTOR TWO. Bilal and Zafar deserve this.

ACTOR ONE. Maybe, but so did they. The nine hundred and fifty who got refused in the last year. Omar, whose full name we can't say, application rejected, Adeniyi Raji sent back to Nigeria on June 29th, Prossy Nakalinzi, who was raped and beaten when sent back. An unnamed person returned to Pakistan after selling a kidney to get here.

And there are so many other unnamed we'll never know, but if it wasn't for chance their names could have been [*Name of* ACTOR ONE.] or [*Name of* ACTOR TWO.] or –

Turns to the audience and asks:

What's your name?

They answer.

And yours?

They answer.

And yours?

They answer.

As ACTOR ONE *speaks to the audience, more names of people* (*in their own voices*) *can be heard through the speakers, building and cascading over each other. The lights get brighter illuminating the audience too, and begin to flicker and pulsate.*

The actors are engulfed by the chorus of names coming from all angles, and when we reach the crescendo –

Blackout.

The End.

A Nick Hern Book

The P Word first published in Great Britain in 2022 as a paperback original by Nick Hern Books Limited, The Glasshouse, 49a Goldhawk Road, London W12 8QP, in association with the Bush Theatre, London

The P Word copyright © 2022 Waleed Akhtar

Waleed Akhtar has asserted his right to be identified as the author of this work

Cover photography by Laurie Fletcher; art direction by Studio Doug

Designed and typeset by Nick Hern Books, London
Printed in Great Britain by Mimeo Ltd, Huntingdon, Cambridgeshire PE29 6XX

A CIP catalogue record for this book is available from the British Library

ISBN 978 1 83904 094 8

Woodland
CARBON
www.woodlandcarbon.co.uk
NICK HERN BOOKS
Printed on Carbon Captured paper

www.nickhernbooks.co.uk

facebook.com/nickhernbooks
twitter.com/nickhernbooks